A SUPERB ALPHABETIC BACKWARD EXPERIENCE

It all begins at the end.

When A is for zebra, Z is for jazz. And all the in-between words start with the last letter, too.

Mark Shulman and Tamara Petrosino, the duo who created *AA Is for Aardvark*, are taking the alphabet apart again. And they've made it more backward than ever!

Look closely, and you'll find all kinds of extra last-letter creatures lurking in the art . . . a manx, a lynx, a kiwi, even a tenrec!

HAPPY ENDINGS!

A is for ZEBRA

By Mark Shulman Illustrated by Tamara Petrosino

STERLING PUBLISHING CO., INC.
NEW YORK

Library of Congress Cataloging-in-Publication Data Available

10 9 8 7 6 5 4 3 2 1

Published by Sterling Publishing Co., Inc.
387 Park Avenue South, New York, NY 10016

Text copyright © 2006 by Mark Shulman
Illustrations copyright © 2006 by Tamara Petrosino
Designed by Joe Bartos

Created at Oomf, Inc.
www.Oomf.com

Distributed in Canada by Sterling Publishing
C/o Canadian Manda Group, 165 Dufferin Street
Toronto, Ontario, Canada M6K 3H6
Distributed in the United Kingdom by GMC Distribution Services,
Castle Place, 166 High Street, Lewes, East Sussex, England BN7 1XU
Distributed in Australia by Capricorn Link (Australia) Pty. Ltd.
P.O. Box 704, Windsor, NSW 2756, Australia

Printed in China
All rights reserved

Sterling ISBN 13: 978-1-4027-3494-6
Sterling ISBN 10: 1-4027-3494-8

For information about custom editions, special sales, premium and
corporate purchases, please contact Sterling Special Sales
Department at 800-805-5489 or specialsales@sterlingpub.com.

N is for Dedication:

For Solomon Leon Shulman, with affection. – M.S.

To Mom and Dad, with love. – T.P.

A is for

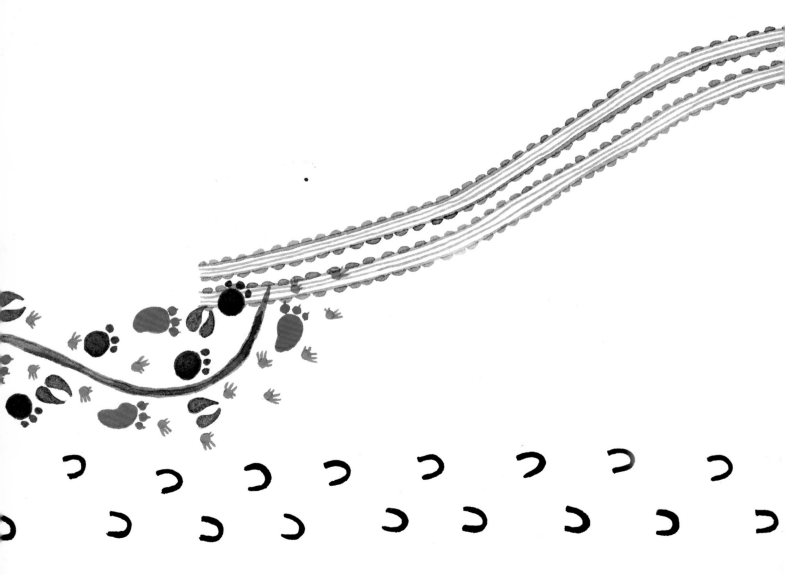

ZEBRA

A is for zebra.

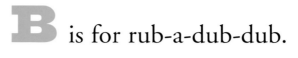
B is for rub-a-dub-dub.

C is for tic and tac, but not toe.

D is for a bald head.

F is for one wolf (but not two).

G is for a juggling peg-leg pig in a wig, dancing a jig on a rug.

H is for itch.

I is for sushi in a deli.

L is for a real cool mackerel.

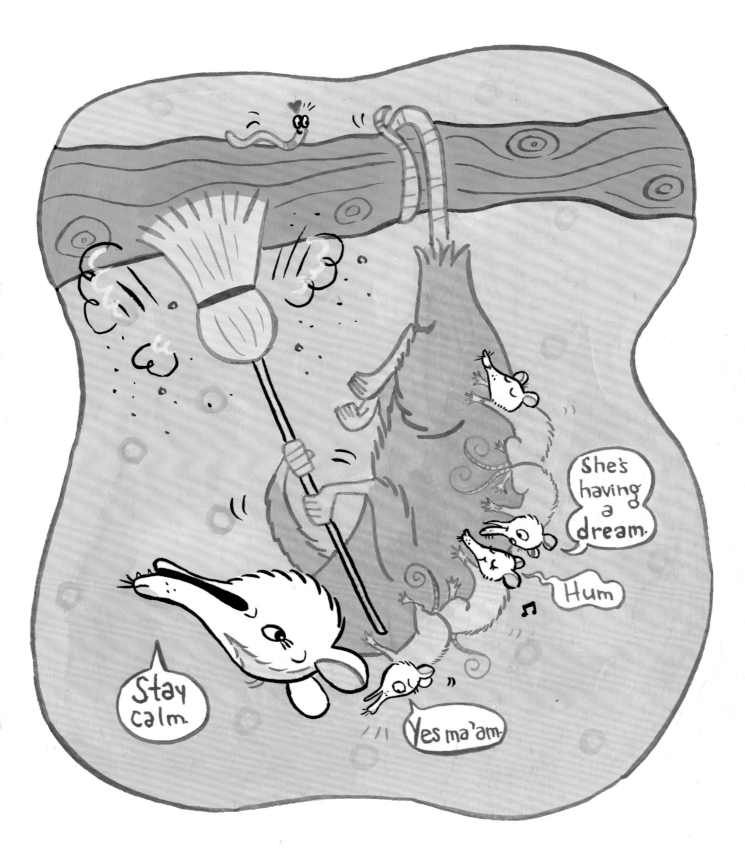

M is for mom.

N is for a green penguin.

O is for Go! Go! Go!

P is for hip-hop.

R is for a four-door car.

S is for the doors.

T is for pat, pet, pit, pot, and put.

U is for a gnu.
The emu in the tutu
helps him through his flu.

V is for TV.

W is for wow! And how!

X is for a chatterbox ox.

Y is for an itty bitty teeny weeny kitty.

Z is for jazz.

Just what a zebra loves to play!

MARK SHULMAN writes for children and adults. He was a camp counselor, a radio announcer, a New York City tour guide, and an advertising creative director before sitting down to write more than 70 children's books. Mark comes from Rochester and Buffalo, NY. Then he moved south, to New York City, where he enjoys many a superb music band—from salsa to jazz.

TAMARA PETROSINO is a graduate of the Rhode Island School of Design. She is the illustrator of *AA Is for Aardvark*, *Rocky the Cat Who Barks*, *How Prudence Proovit Proved the Truth About Fairy Tales*, *There Once Was a Very Odd School*, and *Cat Poems*, as well as many other books for young readers. She resides in New Jersey, and one day will travel the world, from Bologna to Santa Cruz.

STERLING PUBLISHING CO., INC.
NEW YORK

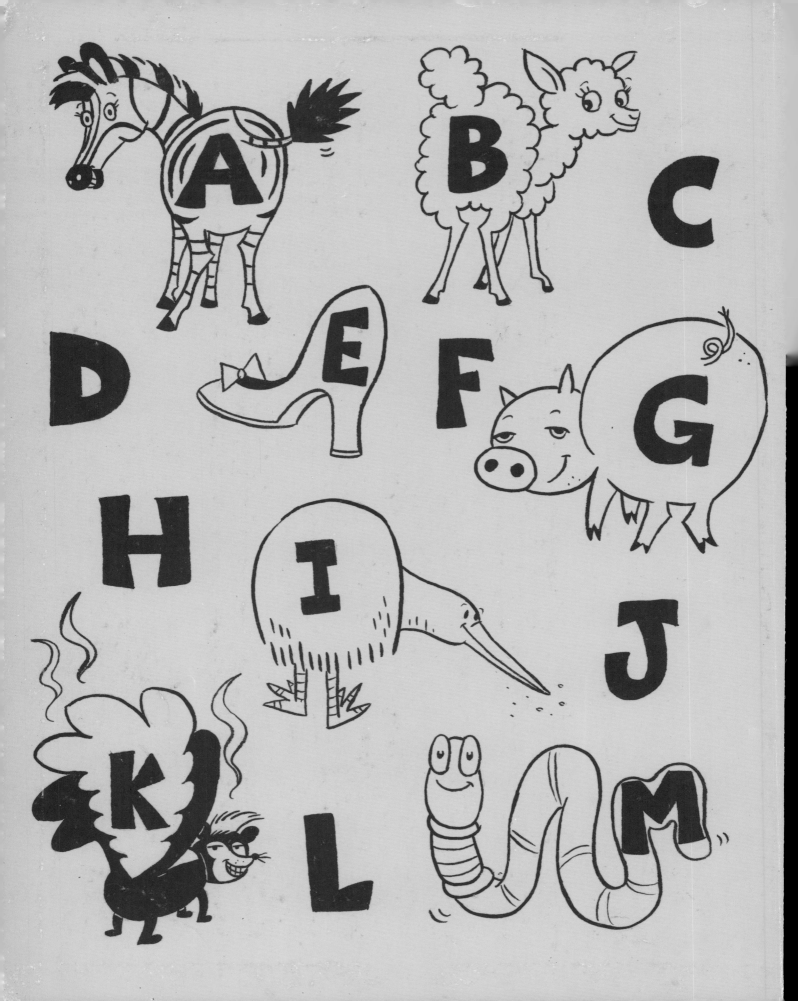